Sanskrit Glossary

for

Self Inquirers

James Swartz

Wewer Keohane, Ph.D.

2018

Cover art: The Essence of OM by Wewer Keohane

James Swartz: www.ShiningWorld.com

Wewer Keohane: www.wewerart.com

Vedanta Invocation Chant

sadashiva samarambhaam
from the first guru, pure existence/consciousness,
shankaracharya madhyamaam
down to Shankaracharya in the midddle
asmad acharya paryantaam
and my teacher at the end
vande guru paramparam
I prostrate to guru-disciple tradition
isvaro guratmeti
Isvara, my guru,
murthi bheda vibaghine
is beyond form and duality
vyomavad vyapta dehaya
beyond space and the body
Dakshinamurthtiyaa namaha
I bow to Isvara in the form of Dakshinamurti, the one who brings self knowledge
sarva vedanta siddhanta
the import of all Vedanta texts
gocharam tamagagocharam
is beyond the known and the unknown
govindam paramanandam
it is limitless bliss and unborn light
satgurum pranatoshmahaam
I worship that reality as my guru

There are many great lessons available on YouTube for deeper pronunciation instruction.

A like the a in about
AA like a in want
Ay like the ay in say
Ai like the a in sand
I like the i in bit
U like the u in put
OO like the a in no
E like the ay in say
EE like the e in meet
AAU like the ow in now
SA as is shh
SAT rhymes with what
NAM rhymes with mom
WAHE sounds like wa-hay
GU sounds like put
Emphasize "ch" like such
V is pronounced softly
Roll the rs slightly

The Sanskrit vowels are, in Sanskrit alphabetical order:
a ā i ī u ū ṛ ṝ ḷ ḹ e ai o au
Of these a i u ṛ ḷ are short, the others are long.
A line over one of a pair of vowels distinguishes long from short.
Source: Sanskrit Dictionary by Denton

Pronunciation

a	as u in but		l	lry in jewelry
ā	a in master		m	m in mother
ai	y in my		ṁ	m in hum
au	ou in loud		n	n in not
b	b in bear		ṇ	2nd n in none
bh	bh in abhor		ṅ	ng in sing
c	ch in check		ñ	n in lunch
ch	chh in catch him		o	o in oh
d	d in dice		p	p in put
ḍ	d in drum		ph	ph in uphill
dh	dh in adhere		r	r in red
ḍh	dh in red-haired		ṛ	ri in river
e	a in evade		ṝ	ri in reed
g	g in good		ś	sh in sure
gh	gh in loghouse		ṣ	sh in show
h	h in hard		s	s in sit
ḥ	h in oh		ṭ	t in water
i	i in fix		t	t in true
ī	ee in feel		th	th in fat-head
j	j in jam		ṭh	th in anthill
jh	dgeh in hedgehog		u	u in suit
k	k in kite		ū	oo in pool
kh	kh in blockhead		v	w in water
l	l in love		y	y in you

Sanskrit Glossary for Self-Inquirers

Sanskrit: 1. an ancient Indic language of India, in which the Hindu scriptures and classical Indian epic poems are written and from which many northern Indian languages are derived.

 A

abadya: what can never be negated or dismissed i.e. the self

abasa vada: the semblance theory, that the reflections of consciousness, all the objects in existence, are apparently real. It is the essence of Shankaracharya's statement, "*brahma satyam jagan mithya*"

abinivesha: love of life

adharma: behavior that is contrary to the natural and moral order; not proper

adita-irdaya: prayers to Sun God

adhyasa: projection, attributing a quality to an object that is not there

adstra-phala: the unseen results of prayer; karma; Grace

advaita: non-dual

advitiya: non-dual

agama: revealed scriptures

adyaropa: superimposition, similar to projection, mixing up the qualities of two things which causes confusion, the self and the body, for instance

agami karma: actions performed with a sense of doership that will rebound to the doer at a later time. *aham brahma*

agni: fire; source of light, not heat

asmi: "I am limitless awareness": a *mahavakya, 'great statement'*

ahamkara: ego, the 'I' notion

aisvarya: overlordship, an attribute of Isvara who controls all objects

ajnana: ignorance, in the context of Vedanta ignorance of one's self as consciousness

akarta: actionless, a word describing awareness

akasa: Space, the first element to evolve from macrocosmic *tamas*

amrta: that which is not subject to death; immortal

anaadi: beginningless, eternal; perpetual,

ananda: bliss, fullness; the spatial limitlessness of you; Kevala Nirvikalpa Samadhi

anandamayakosa: the bliss sheath; the Causal Body, bliss and other mental modifications in seed form *ananta*: limitless*Ananya prema:* exclusive love of Self/Lord

anatma: not-self i.e, the three bodies and the five sheaths

anirvalya: not real or unreal (like a dream)

annamayakosa: the food sheath; the Gross Body

antahkarana: the Subtle Body: mind, intellect, ego and memory

Antaryami: *Isvara*; the Lord; the Inner Controller, sometimes spelled *antaryamin*

anubhava: experience

anvaya: what is essential; "that without which a thing is not a thing," invariable

anvaya vyatireka: elimination of non-essential variables

apana: excretion and the power in the *pranamayakosa* to eject the Subtle Body from the physical body at the time of death

aparokshajnana: direct knowledge

apavada: negation, a method of negating objects

apohana: suspension of the ego (personality); and suspension of thought; often by grace

apta vakya: the testimony of a competent unbiased witness, the Vedanta scriptures

apurushaya: revealed knowledge, beyond human logic

arambha parinama: a "real" transformation: a substance is changed into another substance, milk to cheese, for instance

asangatva: non-attachment

asat: non-existence

asmita: ego

asti: existence, isness

asura: a spirit; not God

atma: the self; atman (the microcosmic self)

atmananda: the bliss of the self

atmanivedana: belonging to the Lord; offering oneself to a deity; self-surrender

avantara vakya: the Vedanta teachings that prepare the mind for the revelation of non-duality

avarana: concealment; denial

avarana Shakti: power of concealment inherent in *Maya*

avasta: state; stage

avicheda vada: the teaching that *jiva* is similar to the space within a pot, in contrast to all-pervasive space; expounded by the Bhamati School of Vedanta

avidya: personal ignorance of the self; of one's true nature

ayam atma brahma: "this self is limitless": a *mahavakya*

ayatana: home as in: the gross body is home for the subtle body

Baudika Prapancha: the Cosmos

bhaga tyaga lakshana: discrimination between the primary meaning of a word and the implied secondary meaning

bhaga tyaga vritti: a discriminating thought

Bhagavan: *Isvara*, the possessor of six forms of spiritual wealth, the creator, sustainer and destroyer of the universe

bhakti: worship; devotion

bhargas/bhargo: radiant light

bhavana: thought, contemplation, dedication

bheda-abheda sambanda: the same but different, Maya. For instance, it is not the same as the self but it is not different from the self either

bhoga: experience, enjoyment

bimba chaitanya: pure original consciousness

Brahman: the limitless self when referred to as the essence of creation; Brahma loka

Brahmancarya: inquiry into the nature of Brahman. Brahma sutras *brahmananda*: the bliss of awareness

Brahmanubhava: existence/consciousness as pure experience

Bramandam: the cosmic egg, the thoughts that create the universe

Brahmavid: knower of Brahman; science of reality

buddhi: intellect, the discriminating function

C

chaitanya: limitless consciousness

chidabasa: reflected consciousness, the Subtle Body

chit/cit: consciousness; the inner immortal essence of every individual, also called the self/Atman

chit chaturvidya prakriya: the teaching of fourfold consciousness

chitjyoti: self lulminous Being; consciousness (sat-chit)

chitta: matter

*E*

eka: one

eva: only

Ganesha: remover of obstacles who broke off one of his tusks so the sruti could be written: non-dual (one tusk)

gandha: odor

gatihi: movement

gayatri: sacred text (see chant between text and glossary

go: cow, earth, words

golaka: sense instruments

grahana: receive, reception

guna: quality: sattva, rajas, tamas; the three energies; rope

guru: 'the one who removes ignorance,' the self, a teacher of Vedanta; a revealer

dama: control of the senses: one of the qualifications for inquiry

devata: Godhead

dharana: concentration in yoga philosophy; a steady mind brought about by the realization of the self in every thought as as redefined by Shankaracharya in Aparokshanubhuti

dharma: behaviors that are in accordance with the natural and moral orders; virtuous behavior; that which akes a thing or being what it is; the law of Being, i.e.: dharma of fire is to burn; dharma of sun is to shine

dharma-megha samadhi: a rain cloud of dharma, nirvikalpa Samadhi, because it purifies the mind

dhyana: meditation in yoga philosophy; the independence from objects brought about by the complete confidence in the thought, "I am limitless awareness" as redefined by Shankaracharya in Aparokshanubhuti

dosha: impurity i.e. *rajas* and *tamas*

dravya Shakti: power of inertia, dullness

drsta-phala: the seen result from prayer; karma

dukka: suffering

dvaita: duality

dvesa: dislikes, hatred, hostility

H

Hari-kiri: destroyer of the poet; literally: disembowelment

Hiranyagarbha: "the Golden Egg"; Isvara identified with all the subtle bodies; the Macrocosmic Subtle Body

hridaya: the heart; what is essential; the self.

I

iccha Shakti: willpower, desire

iccha prarabdha: *karma* that results from acting out desires

idam: "this", defined in this text as "the objects appearing in consciousness"

indriya: organs

Isvara: the Creator; the Macrocosmic Causal Body; the self in association with *Maya*

J

jagan mithya vasana: deep impression (*vasana*) that the world is apparently real.

jagat: the world

jagat karana; the Creator of the world

japa: meditation practice in which a conscious thought of the self replaces worldly thoughts and the space between the repetitions is gradually expanded to reveal reflected consciousness

jiva: living being; the individual self

jiva Paramatma aikyam: the identity of the individual self and the self in everything

jivanmukta: a liberated *jiva* who is no longer identified with objects

jivanmukti: liberation while living

jivatma: living being; the individual self, non-separate from the limitless all-pervading self (*jivo brahmaiva na parah*)

jnana: knowledge, can be worldly knowledge of self knowledge

jnana Shakti: the power of knowledge to transform one's life

jnana avasta: a state of pure objectless experience and knowledge *jnanindriyas*: the five cognitive senses

jyotirjyotih: the light of light; Self

K

karana: cause

karana karya vada: cause and effect, the teaching that the world, the effect, is non-different from its uncaused cause, limitless consciousness

karana sarira: the Causal Body

karika: concise statement of doctrines; commentary, treatise

karma: action

karma phalam: the results of action

karmindriyas: organs of action

karta: doer/enjoyer entity; a motivating thought in the Subtle Body

karya: effect; product

kevala: absolute; doctrine of the absolute unity of spirit; the highest possible knowledge

kasaya: dormant, subconscious trait

kosas: the Five Sheaths; the five layers of the human personality which apparently hide awareness

krama mukti: the theory that *moksa* is attained in stages

kriya Shakti: power of action

krpa: Grace

ksetra: the field: jivatman

ksetrajna: the knower of the field; paramatman

kumbhaka: 'concealed within' in yoga philosophy; steadiness of mind as per Shankara's redefinition of the steps of yoga in Aparokshanubhuti

kutasta: the 'anvil' or the substrate of all experiencing entities i.e. consciousness (from the *jiva*'s perspective)

Lakshmi: Goddess of abundance.

laksana: attribute

lakshyartha or laksharta: implied meaning

laya: mental inactivity; sleep

linga sarira: that by which something is known, a sign, indicator

Mahabharata: epic story: Lotus of the Gita

madu: honey; ego

mahabhutani: the Great Elements: space, air, fire, water, earth

mahatma: a great soul; a Vedantic sage

mahavakya: statements that indicate the identity of the self and the *jiva*

mala: removing impurity particularly *rajas* and *tamas*

manana: the second stage of inquiry: removing doubts about what has been unfolded; reflection on the teachings

manas: mind

mandukya prakriya: the three-state teaching, elimination of the three states as non-essential variables that reveals the self to be the ever-present substrate.

manomayakosa: the mind sheath; the doubting mind (*vimarshatma*), the five *jnanindriyas,* the emotional function.

mantra: sacred revealing words

marga: seeking maura (sllence)

Maya: Ignorance; a power dependent on the self that makes creation possible, composed of the three *gunas*. It is neither the same as the self nor is it different from the self *(sat-asat vilakshanam)*

Mayavada: Non-Dualist School of Vedanta that explains how duality appears without compromising the non-dual nature of the self

mithatva: the quality of being apparent; "seemingness,"

mithya: what is apparently real i.e. all the objects gross and subtle that appear in consciousness/awareness

moda: the *vritti* that creates the happiness that arises in the Subtle Body when a desired object is within one's reach

moksa: liberation; standing in oneself alone; mukti, freedom

mulavidya: root ignorance, Maya

mulabandha: restraining the root

mumukshutva: burning desire for freedom: a primary qualification for inquiry

nama: name

namaskara: surrender ego to Isvara

nididhyasana: the third stage of inquiry: assimilation; obsessively dwelling on the teachings; after karma yoga; removing concepts you had of yourself before you knew you were Self; I am whole and complete; meditation is ongoing; your unconscious issues resolve; letting go of results

nidra: sleep

nirguna: without properties or qualities

nirvana: in Buddhism, a thought free mind in which there is no sense of a separate self

nirvikalpa: non-dual; free of thoughts, differences, division

nirvikalpa samadhi: a state of pure objectless experience and knowledge; a state in which all sheaths, including the bliss sheath, are absent; a state of total absorption in the self

niskama karma: acting with detachment, without motives; actionless action

*nivrtt*i: getting rid of

niyama: the continuous flow of the self-thought to the exclusion of all other thoughts as per Shankara's redefinition of the steps of yoga in Aparokshanubhuti

nyaya: logic, a school of philosophy

nyayika: logician

Om

OM: **Om** is the most sacred symbol in **Hinduism**. In **Sanskrit** known as praṇava " to sound out loudly" or oṃkāra .**Hindus** consider Aum to be the universal name of the Lord and that it surrounds all of creation. Om is the essence that encompasses the three states, waking (A), dreaming (U) and deep sleep (M) , as well as Maya & Consciousness. Pronounced as Om. In **Vedanta**, Om is Self; Brahman.

Omkara: Another term for Om and *Omkara* is pranava, meaning " life force". The ancient yogic texts, such as the *Upanishads, "*The Yoga *Sutras* of Patanjali" and the Bhagavad Gita, mention a method of meditation called Pranava yoga. In this type of yoga and meditation, one concentrates on the sacred sound of the Om mantra, which is believed to represent *Brahman,* or Absolute Reality.

Om Namo Bhagavate Vasudevaya: mantra meaning Bow to Self

pancha kosa vilakshana: free of the Five Sheaths, the self

papa: unfavorable karma brought on by violating dharma; demerit

parabda karma: desire to know the truth

param: the limitless

parama prema svarupa: limitless unconditional love: the nature of the self

paramanus: elementary particles

paramarthika: the perspective of the self

paramatma: the self, limitless consciousness; the inner self of all bodies; ksetrajna; the knower of the field; spirit

parameshwara: supreme Lord; Isvara

paraprakriti: the self, pure existence, as opposed to *aparaprakriti*, pure macrocosmic *tamas, the substance from which all objects are created*

parechada prarabdha: *karma* resulting from the others' desires

parinama karya: actual change, milk to cheese, for instance

paroksha: that which is beyond the range of sense perception, give rise to indirect knowledge

parokshajnana: indirect knowledge

phala: result of karma (what you do)

pragnyanam brahma: "pure original consciousness is limitless", a *mahavakya*

prajna: the sleeper; the *jiva* identified with the Causal Body

prakarana text: an analysis and discussion of *Upanishad mantras*

prakriti: nature; matter in its seed form, the substance from which objects evolve

prakriya: teaching methodology; technique, i.e. applying the opposite thought (diminishes duality)

pralaya: dissolution of the whole universe

prama: the knower; true knowledge

pramana: a means of self-knowledge i.e. Vedanta, an instrument of knowledge (senses, mind and intellect)

pramata: the knower

prameya: object of knowledge

pramoda: the *vritti* that causes the happiness that arises from contact with a desired object *prana*: the vital air; respiration (physiological function); vitality; energy

pranamayakosa: the vital air sheath; the portion of the Subtle Body that is composed of the five vital airs and the five organs of action

pranava: See OM

pranayama: restraint of modifications of the mind as per the redefinition of the steps of *yoga* by Shankaracharya

prarabdha karma: the results of past actions that can only be exhausted as they fructify in this life

pratibandakas: impediments, obstructions

pratibhasika state: subjective reality, the individual *jiva*'s interpretation of reality

pratibhasika satya: the individual *jiva*'s internal world which the *jiva* takes to be a real world

pratibimba: reflection

pratibimba chaitanya: reflected consciousness, i.e. prakriti (the macrocosmic Subtle Body)

pratibimba vada: the teaching that *jiva* is consciousness reflected in three bodies, and *Isvara* is consciousness reflected in the creation; expounded by the Vivarana School of Vedanta

pratipaksha bhavana: applying the opposite thought, a method of negating a particular concept *pratyakatma*: essence of the Subtle body, i.e. awareness

pratyaksha: that which is perceptible by the senses i.e. material objects

pravrti: striving for something

priya: the *vritti* that cause the happiness arising from the thought of a desired object

punya: favorable karma brought on by a life that conforms to dharma; merit

puraka: 'breathing in' as defined in yoga; the thought, "I am the self" as as redefined by Shankaracharya in Aparokshanubhuti

puran bimba chaitanya: original consciousness

purna: the fullness of awareness

purusha: consciousness; knower of the field; spirit; jiva wrapped in matter

raga: harmony; melody

raga-dwesha: likes and dislikes; attraction and repulsion

raja malina: the impure projecting power of *rajas*

rajas: on the level of the macrocosm, the power that transforms material substance (*tamas*) in accordance with the blueprint of the universe contained in macrocosmic *sattva*; on the level of the individual, the doing function and the projecting function; dust

ram: essence; the one who shines in you; Om

rechaka: breathing out in yoga; the negation of the phenomenal world as redefined by Shankaracharya in Aparokshanubhuti

rsi: sage; seer

rupa: form

sadhana: spiritual practice

saguna: possessing properties, with qualities

saksi: the self in the form of the illuminator; the witness *saksi chaitanya*: the non-experiencing witness consciousness as opposed to the experiencing witness consciousness, reflected awareness, the Subtle Body

sama: control of the mind: one of the qualifications for inquiry

samadhana: inner poise; equipoise; persistent focus: one of the qualifications for inquiry

samadhi: the constant bliss of awareness; the non-attachment to thought brought about by the complete identification with the thought, "I am the self, limitless awareness"

samana: assimilation (physiological function)

samana chit: unqualified awareness

samasti: universe

samatva: clarity

samsara: the pursuit of happiness through contact with objects; the belief that the duality caused by *Maya* is real.

samsari: a doer/enjoyer; a *jiva* identified with action and objects

samskara: a deeply-rooted *vasana* or a constellation of *vasanas* that comprise a character trait; complex; caused by gunas/desires

samvit: consciousness; invariable

sanchita karma: the store of karma in the Causal Body waiting to fructify

sankalpa: resolution; prayer; intention

sannyasa: complete renunciation of worldly concerns

sarira*: cause of an experience*

sastra: scripture, any sacred book or composition of divine authority; teaching

sat: existence

sat-asat vilakshana: other than what is real and what is non-existent; seemingly real

satchitananda: the self: existence/eternity, consciousness/limitless awareness, freedom from change (bliss); not subject to time; the content of everything, no beginning and no ending

satori: in Buddhism, sudden enlightenment

satsanga: association with the wise; spiritual discourse

sattvika vrittis: subtle thoughts of the *anandamayakosa* that reflect awareness

sattva: on the level of the macrocosm, the power that provides the intelligence, the design of the creation; on the level of the individual, the power of knowledge and revelation

satya (sattya): what is real; existence/consciousness;Self

savamtva: selfness

savikalpa: with thought

savikalpa samadhi: fixing the mind on the reflection of the self in the Subtle Body, a state of mind in which all thoughts have equal value

sayujya: complete loss of ego

Shakti: power, energy

Shanti: peace

shosaha guna: dehydration

shraddha: faith pending the result of inquiry: one of the qualifications for inquiry

shunya: non-existence

Shunyavada: the school of nihilistic Buddhism

siddhigranta: advanced texts

smriti: secondary texts; Veda-based writings; remembered and handed down in writing

soma: liquor; nectar as offering

sparsa guna: touch

sraddha: having faith, believing in, trusting, faithful, having confidence

sravana: the first stage of inquiry: systematic unfolding; hearing and understanding, an open non-judgmental mind

sri: wealth; diffusing light or radiance

srimat: glorious; endowed with glorious ness; used as a benevolent describer

sristi: creation; the *jiva*'s subjective experience

sruti: scripture (heard); Vedic literature: revelation, the Veda, word of the Lord, hearing, listening. The Veda as eternally heard by certain holy sages thus differing from smrti

sudhi: partaker of the "milk of the Gita (louts)"

sukha; sukka: pleasure; comfort

suksma: intangible; the subtle all-pervading Spirit; Supreme Soul (suksma sarira – subtle body; sthula-gross body)

suksma vrittis: subtle impressions left over from experiences, *vasanas*

svadharma: doing one's God-given duty: one of the qualifications for inquiry; one's true nature

svarupa: true nature: the essential nature of Brahman, reality, saccidananda, true nature of being

svarupavisranti: resting in one's own essential nature

svayamvedana: spontaneous consciousness

T

Taijasa: the "shining one"; the dreamer; the jiva identified with the Subtle Body; originating from or consisting of light (tejas) bright

tamas: on the level of the macrocosm, substance; on the level of the individual, inertia and concealment; denial

tanmatras: Five Subtle Elements-air, space, fire, earth, *water*

tapas: discipline; stand alone; ;intelligent methods of self control

tat tvam asi: "You are That," i.e. the identity of the self and the *jiva*: a *mahavakya*

tattvas: eternal truths, forces and laws

titiksha: forbearance: one of the qualifications for inquiry

tripti: total fulfillment

turiya: 4th factor (some say 4th state, but Vedanta says it is not a state but it encompasses the 3 states), Om, consciousness, true nature

tyaga: to reject the primary meaning of a word and take the secondary, implied meaning; renouncing, abandoning ego, vasanas, world. What a sannyasa must do after self-realization. (self-actualization)

Upanishads: *scripture revealed to the mahatma: sruti*

udana: the physiological power to eject waste from the body, the power that ejects the Subtle Body from the Gross Body at the time of death.

upadesa: restoring an object nearest to its true and proper place

upadhi: something that makes an object appear to be something other than what it is. The blueness in a blue sky is an upadhi. It makes the clear sky seem to be blue. Green glass makes the water look green. Maya at work.

upasana: worship; meditation; being near the adored

uttama adhikari: a highly-qualified inquirer

Vedas: revelations heard by ancient sages; last four, oldest of the Upanishads: Vedanta.

vairagya or viragya: dispassion: one of the qualifications for inquiry

Vaisvanara: Hiranyagarbha, the total mind, identified with the totality of Gross Bodies

vaktartha: ostensible meaning

vasana: inclination that produces action; subtle impression produced by actions that are stored in the Causal Body and produce more actions; the impression of anything remaining unconsciously in the mind, the present consciousness of past perceptions, latent tendencies, idea, imagination, liking, respectful regard; likes/dislikes; fears/desires

vasana kshaya: a yoga concept, a mind not under the influence of the vasanas, a 'dissolved' or empty mind. A belief that enlightenment is no mind.

vasananda: the bliss arising in a calm mind from *vasanas* born from experiencing the self as it reflects in the mind. The bliss that arises in the mind when a *jiva* gets what it wants.

Vasishadvaita: Qualified Non-Dualist School of Vedanta

vastutva: reality

vayu dharma: the nature of Air

Vedanta: Science of Self Knowledge, based on the Vedas.

vega: momentum; force; kinetic energy

vichara/vicara: self-inquiry; consideration, reflection, discrimination, mode of acting or proceeding, investigation, examination, discrimination between the real and the unreal

videha mukti: the theory that *moksa* is attained at death

vidya: knowledge

vignanamayakosa: the intellect sheath and the organs of perception. The discriminating function, intellect (*buddhi*)

vijnana: pure, changeless Consciousness

vijvikalpa: a thought; the oscillating condition of the mind as to the true nature of the thing known

vikara: product; modification

viksepa: projection, mental agitation, inattention

vimarshatma: the doubting mind

viparyaya: the reversal of subject and object brought about by Maya, Macrocosmic Ignorance

Virat: Macrocosmic Gross Body

virya: the capacity to create, sustain and resolve, virility, strength

visesa: distinction, difference; a word which defines or limits the meaning of another word; essence

visesa chit: qualified awareness

vishayananda: the bliss experienced through objects

Viswa: the waking state entity, either a *jivanmukti* or a *samsari*

viveka: discrimination; separating one's pure original consciousness from the Subtle Body, the experiencing entity; not confusing the self with the objects appearing in it. The power of separating the truth from untruth: what is and is not.

viveka dhristi: discrimination between existence and the seven classes of created objects appearing in it *vivesa:* situational dharma (doing what is correct for the particula situation)

rvivarta karya: an apparent change: an effect that appears to be different from its cause.

vivarta parinama: an apparent transformation i.e. the creation

vritti: sentient thought mode; experience; the process of knowing; whatever is happening in the intellect

vrittijnana: thought

vyana: circulation (physiological function)

vyapti: universal rule without an exception; omnipresence

vyasa: sage (wrote Gita) with the help of Ganesha

vyatireka: non-essential; what is incidental

vyavaharika: the empirical world

yajna: sacrifice, worship, devotion, act of worship, devotion, prayer

yama: control of the senses

yasas: fame

yoga: to join or yoke. The complete absorption of the mind in the thought, "I am awareness and not the body-mind/sense complex" as redefined by Shankaracharya in Aparokshanubhuti.   Vedanta is 'the yoga of no-contact' i.e. self knowledge.

yoga nidra: *Isvara*'s sleep, a state of 'conscious sleep.' State of consciousness between waking and sleeping, like the "going-to-sleep" stage. It is a state in which the body is completely relaxed, and the practitioner becomes systematically and increasingly aware of the inner world by following a set of verbal instructions. This state of consciousness (yoga nidra) is different from meditation in which concentration on a single focus is required. In yoga nidra the practitioner remains in a state of light withdrawal of the 5 senses with four of his or her senses internalized, that is, withdrawn, and only the hearing still connects to the instructions.

yuga: period of time

In gratitude for the Steady Wisdom study group at True
Nature Healing Arts and to Ramji James Swartz.

Wewer Keohane, Ph.D.

Carbondale, Colorado USA

Om tat sat

www.ingramcontent.com/pod-product-compliance
Lightning Source LLC
Chambersburg PA
CBHW072342270726
48659CB00023B/2304